#ThisIsHowWeLive

Exposing how Generation Y feels, loves and creates.

MADDALENA ALECCE

I have tried to recreate events, locales and conversations from my memories of them. In order to maintain their anonymity, I have changed the names of all individuals and in some instances, I may have changed some identifying characteristics to further respect their privacy.

Cover Illustration and Design by Chris Muscari

Cover Design by Davidson Adames

ISBN-10: 0692565922
ISBN-13: 978-0692565926

Per Mamma & Papa', due membri speciali della generazione che ci ha cresciuto.

Se posso vivere cosi, e' anche grazie a voi.

Quanto sono fortunata?

For Mom & Dad, two very special members of the generation who raised us.

The reason why I can live like this is also thanks to you.

How lucky am I?

Maddalena Alecce

ACKNOWLEDGMENTS

I'd like to thank the people who agreed to share their story. Thank you for confiding in me and being so raw, honest and candid. None of this would've been possible without you. You made our voice matter so here's to us, here's to you!

I'd also like to thank my family, or in Generation Y lingo, my hashtag-squad: Luigi Alecce, Camilla Rivetti, Carlo & Sabina Rivetti, Alessia Nava, Renato Besabe, Alessandra Albini, Richard T. McFarland, Marina Serena Cacciapuoti, Franco Falcone, Alessandro Ventura and Fred & Darlene Hunter.

I'm incredibly lucky to have you in my life. You inspire me, support me, teach me valuable life lessons and some of you take up the daunting task of scolding me when needed. Quite simply, you are always there for me.

TABLE OF CONTENTS

one   Letter To The Reader   1

two   This Is How We Work   6

three   This Is How We Create   16

four   This Is How We Advocate   24

five   This Is How We Travel   33

six   This Is How We Communicate   40

seven   This Is How We Date   49

eight   This Is How We Care   60

nine   This Is How We Bail   67

ten   This Is How We Love   75

eleven   & This Is How I Live   88

1 LETTER TO THE READER

Dear Reader,

I was strongly advised not to start like this but here I am doing it anyway. I can't help myself because if you're reading this I owe you a big thank-you because you just purchased a book written by someone who has no endorsements whatsoever.

Like most people featured in these essays, I am still a work-in-progress. I am no expert on anything because I'm still learning everything and the only thing I feel comfortable calling myself, is an observer with a bunch of thoughts.

I am a Generation Y member, a Millennial, a twentysomething – whatever term you want to use for the cohort of individuals born between the 1980's and mid-2000's – and I wrote this book for you, however old you are and whichever generation you belong to.

Before telling you what #ThisIsHowWeLive is, allow me to tell you everything it is not. This collection of essays is not about wanting to change your mind on anything; it is not about wanting to prove how one generation might be better or worse than the other and it most definitely is not about stigmatizing any generation or individual who is part of it.

#ThisIsHowWeLive is meant to do one thing, and one thing only: expose us, in all our rawness. It's something written by us, about us, for you. It's about showing you the flip side of the coin and you can make of this information what you want.

I'd like you to think of these essays as a naked body. Someone's face *sans* make-up; someone's stomach with no abs; someone's breasts with no bra. You get the drift, right?

I spent months meeting, talking and connecting with people in all five boroughs. I didn't discriminate and paid no attention to race, ethnicity, sexual orientation, social or economic class.

Some readers will claim these are all relevant factors and I would agree with them. But to fulfill the objective of this book, I deemed all the aforementioned irrelevant because I was not trying to identify patterns amongst Generation Y based on what makes us different. I was trying to identify patterns that make us somewhat similar to one another, a united group if you will, regardless of ethnicity, race and social standing.

I tried to include, to the very best of my ability, all of it. The good and the bad, the virtues and the sins, the beautiful and the ugly. I quoted thoughts and opinions of individuals who truly forced me to think how we twentysomethings live and hopefully, their words will provoke a response from you too.

I spoke to hundreds of people and to protect their anonymity I have changed their names, and in some instances, even identifying characteristics. What I haven't changed however, are their words and thoughts, which are not scripted, edited or polished in any way. You'll read their stories the same way I heard them.

Chances are you will agree with some and disagree with others. You will find some coherence but you will also find a lot of inconsistency and contradiction. It's just part of the package.

It's important to point-out that the chapters in this book are independent to themselves so I suppose you could read them in any order. My suggestion however, would be to read them in the sequence you find them. By the time you get to the last one, you will realize there is nothing random about their order.

Think of these essays like an iceberg. I'd like you to start looking at the tip first and discover the depth and width of it all as you keep reading.

But before you do any of that, I want to get one last thing straight.

I beg to differ with the common belief that Generation Y is spoiled, entitled and somewhat shallow.

We aren't spoiled. Most of us were fortunate enough to be raised in an era where change can happen and choices matter.

We aren't entitled. We were taught to go after what we want and not waste time on what we don't.

We are by no means shallow. We are a generation that fights for equality rights, human rights, animal rights, any type of right, just as much as the generations that preceded us.

So as you read this, consider the possibility that maybe the hype surrounding Generation Y has nothing to do with a date of birth. Maybe, it has everything to do with the fact that we have different tools to express those same ideals and feelings that make us a civilization, a society, just human beings really.

We picked up where older generations left off. And this is how we do it, this is how we live.

2 THIS IS HOW WE WORK

There is no in between. No grey area. When it comes to Generation Y in the workplace, it's either black or white. Some employers love us and others absolutely dread us.

I've met managers who were incredibly eager and psyched to hire us. In fact, they couldn't wait to have a little army of twentysomethings tweeting and hashtagging about their company. But I also met some who were absolutely terrified at the thought of hiring someone who takes pictures of their lattes, tweets about their daily commute and can't seem to entertain a conversation without constantly checking their phone.

What gives?

I was having drinks with a friend in his mid-thirties, when he started complaining about one of his employees, a young lady in her twenties, who had recently expressed her need for praise whenever she did something that exceeded my friend's expectations.

"Well, that sounds fair to me," I told him. "Why wouldn't you want to praise someone when they do a good job? It's encouraging, they'll feel good about themselves and keep up the good work."

My friend didn't quite agree. His argument, which I have found is pretty common when it comes to how we work, was that, in his day and age, there was no such thing as a praise or as some call it, "instant gratification."

You just did what you were told and doing it right didn't get you a gold star. It just meant you were doing your job.

"You're not in kindergarten anymore," my friend concluded.

Three days later, I was wandering around the Financial District when I ran into Cristina, 25, junior analyst at an investment banking firm.

"I work in a very corporate environment. I wear pencil skirts and silk blouses because that's what I'm supposed to do, but things are starting to change," she said.

When I asked Cristina to elaborate she told me how she had recently landed a very large account with a phone-app start-up company.

"Our VP had been after that company for a while but for one reason or the other, the deal was never sealed. I don't have his expertise in the field, but I do know how to talk to twentysomethings and that's exactly what the CEO of the start-up was."

Despite Cristina's lack of experience, she figured the way to land an account like that was not by wearing a suit and talking business within the walls of a conference room.

She met the founder of the company, apparently a very good looking twenty-eight year old man, at a trendy bar for happy hour. She wore ripped jeans and her favorite pair of kicks instead of a pencil skirt. She bonded first and talked business later, and somehow, three weeks later, a prospective client turned into an account.

According to Cristina, her boss did not investigate how she managed to land the account. Maybe, as my friend had explained to me, it didn't really matter because she had just done her job. That doesn't get her a gold star, right?

But actually, Cristina is a prime example of how, sometimes, our unconventional ways will still achieve the desired result.

This is not to say that we should all start showing up at staff meetings with hoodies and sneakers. It simply means that, what we lack in experience, we make up with the ability to identify when being our twentysomething self can be advantageous in the workplace.

That day I walked away thinking that maybe Millennials shouldn't be labeled as inappropriate or unprofessional. Our lingo, style and casual way of approaching things can benefit an employer, especially today, a day and age where, company founders are younger than ever.

As far as praising us is concerned, I guess we should be praised when we do something right. But when we aren't, it's okay too. Our Twitter followers will gladly retweet our accomplishment of the day and just like that, we'll be instantly gratified.

———————————

Not too long ago, I graduated college and started interviewing for a number of jobs in the marketing field. It didn't take long for me to notice a trend: the younger the interviewer, the more they seemed to like me. And I use the word "seemed" because of course, looks can be deceiving.

But assuming I'm right, it was very clear to me that the vibe between a twenty-six year old and I was completely different than the one between me and a forty-two year old.

The twenty-six year old asked me questions like, "How would you use social media to promote Product X? Which visuals would you pick for our brochure? Which one of your extra-curricular activities has prepared you most for this job?"

The forty-two year old, on the other hand, asked questions like, "What makes you the perfect candidate for this job? How has your course of study prepared you to work with us? Where do you see yourself five years from now?"

The more interviews I went to, the more I realized that the twentysomethings were asking me questions related to the job itself, the "what would you do if" kind of questions, whereas the fortysomethings were asking me questions that were geared towards understanding my theoretical preparation and vision for the future.

I pictured the twentysomething thinking, "Does she really know how to use social media for business? Can she come up with shareable content? Is she a people person or did she spend her college years solely on textbooks?"

But I pictured the fortysomething thinking, "Did she graduate knowing the 4P's of marketing? Is she committed to the marketing field or is she going to leave us half-way through training to be a blogger? Does she know email etiquette? Someone check her social media."

A few weeks later, Dave, 54, a Human Resources Director, clarified why I might have felt the way I did during my interviews.

"I employ a lot of recent graduates. But it's so tough with you guys. Most of you leave the company within the first two years. You're not loyal. And we lose money and time training you for what? Our competitors?"

I remembered what Andrew, 24, had told me when I asked him about his first job.

"I left my first job after nine months. Things were going well but I got an offer from a company that shared my vision. So I left. Why not?"

The more twentysomethings I spoke to after that, the more obvious it became that Andrew wasn't the only one.

The thing is, it's not that we are not loyal. But in the words of Samantha Jones "we love you, but we love ourselves more."

Why shouldn't we? What exactly are we being accused of? Taking chances? Striving for more? Growing out of something and moving on to something better?

If wanting to take advantage of the sea of opportunity that lies ahead of us makes us unfaithful, then I guess, so be it. In fact, maybe Dave is right; we might just be sluts.

But before resenting us, please consider the possibility we are only doing what our fifth grade teacher drilled in our heads. We're thinking outside the box because #YOLO[1]. Don't worry though, we will not unfollow your company. We are loyal to the ones we follow and who have followed us.

------

[1] #YOLO: a hashtag commonly used on social media as an abbreviation for "You Only Live Once."

It was sometime in March when I was in line at Whole Foods and overheard (I was eavesdropping, whatever) a man calling whom I assumed was his son.

"Why are you picking up Christopher? Aren't you at work? I was going to leave you a voicemail."

I don't know what Christopher responded but I think it's safe to assume he said the same thing I tell my mom when she calls me and I pick up at work.

"You know how many times I told him not to use his phone? Do you use your phone at work?" the man asked me, after he caught me staring at him.

Christopher's dad is not the first person to question our so called "phone addiction" in the workplace. It seems to be one of those topics that just keeps coming up, whether it's at monthly office staff meetings or weekly Sunday dinners with the family.

Here's the deal with our phones and the workplace: we know it's not right but, as arrogant as it sounds, we sometimes feel like it's okay to do it anyway.

We use our phone for pretty much everything, whether it's taking notes, reading emails, buying coffee or listening to music, and the truth is, we wouldn't go more than an hour without checking it or doing something with it. But let's be real folks, that applies to anyone, not just Millennials.

I mean, c'mon, even my mom is now hooked on WhatsApp and will say things like, "You were online at 10:23 p.m., why didn't you respond to my text?"

Nowadays, it's simply unrealistic to expect anyone, regardless of age, to go hours without checking their phone. This is why, when people call us out on it, it really doesn't do much.

Sure, some of us might apologize and maybe put it away for a good half-an-hour but at the end of the day, many of us will walk away knowing that, sooner or later, others will embrace our addiction, the same way we do.

When major news breaks affecting your company and we'll be the first ones to report it back to you, you'll like it. When you'll ask us to promote a party and we manage to start a trending hashtag in a matter of hours, you'll love us. When we bring in a new client or boost your company's image by tweeting someone who knows someone who knows someone else, you'll appreciate us.

I'm not saying we are perfect. We are far from it. We still have a lot to learn and in time, most of us will. And make no mistake, there are times when we do deserve a good scolding for being too casual or unconventional.

But there are also times, when companies would be better off allowing us to work the way we do, because in some instances, like the Cristina's of the world show us, our way works too.

3 THIS IS HOW WE CREATE

As biased as this sounds, I have found that the ideas Millennials come up with are often pretty freaking awesome and practical.

The workforce today is flooded with twentysomethings who are working hard towards becoming the next Steve Jobs. Companies like Facebook, Snapchat, WhatsApp, Tinder and many more were all founded by twentysomethings who, up until a few years ago, only had a somewhat cool idea and maybe a few bucks to invest in it.

Eric's son is one of the many. I bumped into Eric, 47, in Gramercy Park and when I say bumped, I mean that quite literally. I was scrolling down my Instagram feed and walked right into him.

"Watch it," he yelled, "Always on these damn phones!"

His frustration could be sensed a mile away. His son Larry, a twenty-one year old who had recently dropped out of Pace University, was about to launch his new mobile-app.

"I'm not saying what he creates isn't worth his time," Eric explained, "All I'm saying is that you young people think today is all that matters. You have to plan for tomorrow too. College degree, financial security, stable job. Does any of this ring a bell? What if this app thing doesn't work? What if your writing doesn't work, Maddalena?"

If you're a parent, I'm sure you've reprimanded your son or daughter like this at least once and if you're a Generation Y member, I'm one-hundred-percent sure you've heard a version of this multiple times before. I know I have, many many times.

Before parting ways, I asked Eric if I could have his son's phone number.

"Use whatever you guys all use, I'm sure you'll find his contact information plastered somewhere online," he said.

And I sure did. I found Larry on Facebook and spoke to him briefly on the phone.

"Don't get me wrong," he told me, "I love my old man, but I don't feel like I should be in school right now. I'd rather be fighting with my dad over something that I love doing, instead of fighting with him over bad grades for being in school for something I'm not even into."

When Larry and I hung up, I had mixed feelings about the whole thing. Part of me felt he was acting spoiled for not realizing there are millions of people out there who would kill to even have the opportunity to go to college. But the other part of me, knew exactly where he was coming from. The quarrel he was having with his father wasn't any different than the one I had with my own when I decided to move overseas.

I wondered: was Larry being ungrateful or was he being daring and fearless?

———————————

I met Dalia, 25, somewhere between Prince and Mercer Street. She told me she dropped out of law school seven months ago after her parents told her to get her shit together.

"They wanted me to code less and study more. I was doing well in school but I wasn't excelling. I was winging it, but I ended up getting it together."

I assumed she meant she started studying more but that wasn't the case.

"I quit," she confessed. "I started coding full-time and now I work for a video-game company. I spend my days creating and coding surreal environments for people's entertainment. I love it. I am so happy," she told me as she whipped out her phone to show me some of her work.

Dalia's parents weren't happy at first. Her mother, a corporate lawyer, didn't understand why, the same daughter who spent most of her childhood dreaming of becoming a great lawyer now wanted to create video-games.

Her grandfather, gathered tons of articles and research on the top salaries in the gaming industry, hoping to dissuade Dalia from dropping out.

"They felt let down when I broke the news to them. I love what I do and the only regret I have, is going to law school in the first place. I should've trusted my gut. When you love doing something, you never settle. In law school, I was complacent, but ever since I quit I never settled for mediocrity once. I excel, every single day," Daria concluded.

In our early twenties, most of us have a very broad idea of what we want to do and an even broader idea of who we want to be. We end up using a trial-and-error approach and figure things out as we go and most of the times, we let people down in the process. That includes employers, parents, friends and mentors.

We swear by the things we start with such conviction only to end up swearing by something else a few years or sometimes even months later. But at the end of the day, all we're doing is getting to know ourselves.

You see, the way we are perceived has very little to do with the way we feel or what we do and what we end up doing has absolutely nothing to do with how we're perceived by the people around us.

In others words, we don't make decisions because of you or in spite of you. It's usually just about us. We're egotistic like that sometimes.

Two weeks later, I met Amir, 24, a social media coordinator in a Los Angeles based digital media agency. He told me about his passion for photography and the portfolio albums he creates for poets and writers.

Although he majored in communications and gradually shifted in the digital field after interning in Los Angeles and Chicago, he never put photography aside.

I told him about my freelance work as a writer and that's when he asked me why I was writing this book.

"Can't think of a reason not to," I responded.

"You should add that too!"

"Add what?" I asked.

"Add that we don't look for reasons to do something. We look for reasons not to and when we can't think of anything we just do it. Write something about us being bold."

Amir's words forced me to think back to Larry, Dalia and all the other Millennials I ran into. None of them had given me specific reasons why they create what they do but all of them, didn't have any good reason not to go for it.

I realized then, that when I spoke to Larry I had questioned his behavior and maybe I shouldn't have. Not wanting to be in college right now had nothing to do with him being ungrateful.

What if it was just about him wanting to take the risk and believing in his product? And maybe Dalia didn't quit law school wanting to upset her parents. What if she enrolled in the first place because she was trying to avoid disappointing them?

Amir might be right. We are bold. We dabble in majors, internships and jobs and try to make the best of it and when it doesn't work out, we start all over again. Because we believe we can even when the people around us don't. If that's not bold, I don't know what is.

Months later, a friend of mine mentioned a commencement speech delivered by Jim Carrey in May 2014 at Maharishi University of Management.

As I listened to Carrey's speech and anecdotes about his childhood, I heard one passage in particular that perfectly summarizes what I have found to be true amongst Millennials and how we create.

"I learned many great lessons from my father, not the least of which was that you can fail at what you don't want, so you might as well take a chance on doing what you love." - Jim Carrey

I concluded then, that most of us, will listen to your advice but we won't always take it and it's not because we're disrespectful or entitled or delusional.

The truth is, you can hit us with all the statistics you can find and it still won't work. We don't take your advice because we have no idea if what we create is going to work but you don't either. Although we know you've been around the block a few times before us, we also know you don't have a crystal ball and that's how you lose us.

We listen to your opinion, but we treat it as exactly that, an opinion. It has nothing to do with our love or respect for you. In fact, in most cases it has nothing to do with you at all.

It has everything to do with ourselves and the fact that we're willing to take the risk. And here's the kicker: we're cocky enough to console ourselves with the fact that if something doesn't work out, we still have plenty of time to create something else. Something that might.

4 THIS IS HOW WE ADVOCATE

We're nothing like our grandparents. In case you haven't noticed, we will not be sticking to the same laundry detergent for the next thirty years because "that's what we're used to buying."

It's safe to say, we are the exact opposite of that. Not only do we like change. We crave and welcome it with open arms once we find it. I guess that's why, for years, advertising agencies, market researchers and psychologists have been spending millions of dollars trying to figure out how to make us loyal to a product, brand, service or even an idea.

I asked Ron, 46, Marketing Director for a shoe brand, what his thoughts were.

"Millennials are a tough market to penetrate; they don't just buy something because they like it; they actually have to believe in whatever your brand stands for. It goes above and beyond the product itself. If you don't give them a story to tell, it won't work."

Bingo! Glad to see we're not that hard to decipher after all.

Basically, we are social activists. Contrary to popular belief, we are not that selfish or lazy when it comes to the causes we care about and the key to getting us to do anything is to make us feel part of something.

It's not enough for us to walk into a store or visit a website and buy something because we like it. In order for us to go through with a purchase or join a cause, we actually have to relate to it.

It might be hard to believe, but we have a deeply rooted sense of community and anything we buy, engage in, or believe in must be something we wouldn't feel ashamed advocating for. And make no mistake, we want to be advocates.

As a generation who loves sharing everything, story-telling is so instrumental to us. We love to promote something that makes us feel connected to one another and that somehow tells a story so it makes sense that advocacy is a such a huge part of our life.

This all sounds so wonderful, or at least it does to me, but unfortunately, it's not all rainbows and unicorns. As Karen, 39, pointed out to me, our advocacy methods are not always perceived in a good way.

"I'm having a very hard time understanding my daughter. She just turned down two job offers. The first because she 'sensed' there was no room for growth - okay fine. But the second, she turned down because the CEO recently released a statement anti-abortion and she said she didn't want to be associated with a company who didn't respect women's rights," Karen told me.

"What's wrong with that?" I asked her.

"What's wrong is that I am pro-abortion just like her, but I don't use my workplace to advocate for that. Advocate after hours or in the weekends. Work is work, and you shouldn't drag your personal life and opinions in it. It's inappropriate," she concluded.

To that, Karen's husband, Jacob, added, "The media calls you guys the 'Me Generation'. I don't think I agree with that. You're the 'Extreme Generation'. No filters. Many of you still have to learn that there's a right place and time for everything."

————————————————

Karen and her husband forced me to think about the type of advocate I am and how I became one in the first place.

I'm pretty sure, I can track that exact moment back to my freshman year in college, when I had just moved 4,000 miles away from home. I remember that, instead of feeling frightened by the unknown, I was acting like your stereotypical seventeen year old. I was thirsty for independence and excited for all the nights with no curfew I had ahead of me.

Of course, like every freshman usually does, by the time October came around, I learned my hard sought independence had a price and maybe I didn't have it all that bad back home.

Aside from realizing the obvious – things like having to do your own laundry, keeping track of bills and dealing with a demanding schedule all by yourself sucks – I also realized there was one more thing my parents used to do: advocate and campaign for me .

It took flying to the other side of the Atlantic Ocean for me to finally realize that now that I was living alone, I had to stand up for myself, pick my battles and how I was going to fight them. That's when I first started to think of myself as an advocate.

I went from volunteering in correctional facilities, to tutoring students with special needs, to donating time and money to causes I cared about to writing articles on social issues dear to my heart.

The more concerned my mom got over the reasons why I was standing up for causes she never even introduced me to, the more I was shaping myself into becoming the advocate I am today.

I can only assume that's what Karen's and Jacob's daughter was doing too. Can we blame her?

I met Alexis, 21, somewhere in Chinatown. She was with a group of other twentysomethings encouraging pedestrians to join the #PlusIsEqual movement, a campaign launched by retailer Lane Bryant, aiming at equal representation of women of all shapes and sizes.

"You're probably thinking I've got no business advocating for this," Alexis told me when I first approached her.

"Why would you say that? This is actually pretty awesome. I'd advocate for this too," I told her.

"Because I'm a size four. My aunt says I should focus on advocating for something that actually affects me."

"So, why are you here, then?"

"Because this *is* something that affects me. I'm a woman, too. And fine, I'm not a size 14, but I might as well be. Do you ever see a size four on billboards? This affects all of us. And it isn't about advocating for plus size models. It's much more than that. It's about a woman's right to feel comfortable in her own body – whether that's a size 4, 6, 8, 12, whatever. I'm supporting a movement that reminds people that billboards are deceiving. You can be a healthy size zero, if that's your body type, anyway. But you can also be a healthy size 12. It's not about the number, its simply about your shape. Stop trying to shape women into something they're not. Let them thrive in the body they already have. And if that's a plus size, so what?" Alexis said.

The following day, I got invited to a photography studio in Bushwick. There, I met two young male photographers who were working on a series of photographs shot at the arrival and departure terminal of John F. Kennedy Airport.

"The goal was to capture moments of joy and excitement as well as sadness and despair," one of the photographers told me.

I asked him what prompted him and his colleagues to start this project.

"We're raising awareness for LGBT rights. This is how it works: each photograph represents a different feeling and it's up to the buyer to pick a photograph that symbolizes how he or she feels about the LGBT community. It works because we don't force the buyer to support LGBT, instead, we embrace their opinion, whatever that is, but in the meantime, make them aware of the fact that all proceeds go towards LGBT foundations," he told me.

Hundreds of Millennials later, I was reminded of something and went back to what Karen and Jacob had originally told me.

Steve Jobs once said, "You can't connect the dots looking forward; you can only connect them looking backwards. So you have to trust that the dots will somehow connect in your future."

For the most part, I find this statement is true for everyone, but since we're talking about Generation Y, I'm going to go ahead and say it is especially true for us.

What we advocate for and the way we do it, is something most of us do in good faith. Though we don't always know how what we do can make a difference, we are hoping that at some point in the future, our efforts will have been for something.

We are flawed in many ways and as Karen and Jacob pointed out, when we believe in something we don't know where to draw the line and we act in fact as "Generation Extreme."

We'll stop buying products if the brand in question doesn't support a cause we do. We'll quit jobs if the company releases statements we deem unjust. We'll wear shirts and hashtag photos to make our voice heard. We'll march down the street getting as many people involved as we can and maybe not all of this is always right or appropriate.

But when I am reminded of what advocacy really is, or should be anyway, I am also reminded that a true advocate is someone who believes in something so much that the time and place to speak up for it is everywhere, anywhere, at any time.

There's no denying the fact we are a highly educated, opinionated and annoyingly loud generation and we like to leverage all that to promote our beliefs.

Isn't that what distinguishes a great advocate from a mediocre one?

5 THIS IS HOW WE TRAVEL

We're young, full of energy and most of us haven't lived long enough to have faced terrible things, so we are still annoyingly dreamy.

As maddening as we are to our parents, mentors and employers, we still believe in "carpeing the diem." Actually, scratch that. We don't just believe in it. We live by it and traveling has become one of the many ways in which we seize the moment.

Thanks to technological advances, new means of transportation and innovative channels of communication, not only has traveling become easier but it's now also faster and (can be) cheaper than ever.

All these factors combined have enabled Generation Y to build a network of people that consists of family, friends and yes, even followers.

The world is, quite literally, at our fingertips. So, we swipe our credit cards left and right and off we go (irresponsible budgeting, we know). While some people applaud us for our constant traveling, others are skeptical, claiming we're quite foolish and to some extent, unreliable, because of it.

———————

It was a Monday when I met Jean-Paul, 51, at about 7:00 a.m. during my morning commute. He started telling me about his son and daughter, both in their early twenties.

"Those two drive me crazy. How about planning ahead of time instead of purchasing trips on a whim? Just last month my son told me he's going to Melbourne for two weeks. When I asked him where he was going to stay he told me had a friend of a friend he met on Twitter who was going to host him. I had to remind him he has a full-time job and—"

I interrupted him and told him about Marcus, a twenty-year old I met who was working in Argentina and ended up taking a month off to travel around South America.

"See, that's what I'm talking about," Jean-Paul continued.

"You guys are delusional. Let me tell you something. Traveling is important, but if you think you can wing your twenties by hopping on planes you're in for a very rude awakening when you turn thirty and got nothing to show for it, aside from credit card bills and airline miles that is."

A few train stops later, I sat next to Rebecca, 45.

"My daughter lives abroad. Haven't seen her in eight months. I don't know what she's looking for but she better find it soon. Home is here, not backpacking who knows where for god knows how long," she told me.

By the time I got home that night, I was in full panic mode. Jean-Paul had basically ripped me a new one. All I could think about were his ingredients for a stable life, a.k.a. your 401(k), your retirement plan and your savings.

Rebecca, on the other hand, had stressed me out too. She made me wonder whether my parents had felt the same way she was feeling about her daughter, after I started calling New York home, a city an ocean away from where they raised me.

I started to question our behaviors myself. Could it be, that what we think is the norm – moving abroad and hopping from one continent to the other – is actually an irrational and irresponsible behavior?

Are we not planning enough? Are we winging it too much? To the point where we're sabotaging our forty-year old self and dissing our home at the same time?

––––––––

It wasn't until a few weeks later, when I spoke to Grace and Jordan, both 25, that my panic started to subside. I met them at a networking event in Brooklyn Heights.

"I've lived in six countries. So far, I've figured out everything I don't want," Grace told me.

I directed the same question to Jordan and told him about Jean-Paul's point of view.

"I just want to find my place in the world, somewhere I can call home. That's why I travel. Once I find that, I can work on everything else," he said.

"Don't you have a home already?" I asked him, as I replayed Rebecca's words in my mind.

He shook his head. "Traveling is how I'm looking for it. It's not about where your home is, it's about who it allows you to be once you find it."

A few hours later, as I walked the Brooklyn Bridge overlooking the skyline, I thought about all the traveling it took me to find my home, that place that allows me to be who I am. That's when it occurred to me that Jean-Paul's and Rebecca's arguments had a glitch.

When I first spoke to Jean-Paul, he assumed that what Millennials are striving to have by the time they turn thirty is a hefty 401(k), a stable and rewarding job and maybe enough savings for a mortgage.

I'm sure there are plenty of Millennials out there who are after exactly that and there is nothing wrong with them. In fact, those Millennials are better off doing what Jean-Paul says. They should travel when their job and finances allow them to because traveling across the world on a "whim", as he described it, won't help them find that stability they might be looking to have a few years from now.

But what about the other Millennials? What about the Jordan's and Grace's amongst us? Is it fair to label them delusional and assume their traveling habits are damaging their future?

I don't think so. Traveling is all about fulfillment and whatever generation you happen to be part of, I think we can all agree that people travel to satisfy some sort of need.

So in a way, Rebecca is right. We do travel hoping to find something. In some cases that something is ourselves.

Because the thing is, we're not after stability just yet. A home isn't an apartment, a college dorm or a job. As harsh as it might sound, sometimes home isn't even the place where we were raised either.

Home to us are people and the more people we meet, the more sides of ourselves we discover that we never even knew were there in the first place.

So we travel hoping to meet the person we want to become. Once we find out who that is, chances are, we will also have found "our" place. And that's when, all of a sudden, we'll start thinking about Jean-Paul's ingredients for a happy and stable life.

———————

I suppose then, that we're not irresponsible or delusional. The way we travel can be just as rewarding and valuable as it can be damaging.

We all travel with a different purpose in mind and we all have a different wish-list for our thirty or forty year old self.

As far as the concept of home goes, believe us when we tell you that we find pieces of home anywhere we go and leave pieces of us everywhere we go.

Rest assured though, as ungrateful as we might look to you, we never forget where we come from. We're true to our roots, wherever those might be. And that's not even a generation thing. That, I believe, is a universal thing.

6 THIS IS HOW WE COMMUNICATE

At some point in the late 1700's, theologian and philosopher Joseph Priestley wrote that, "The more we elaborate our means of communication, the less we communicate." He had this thought when phones didn't exist, never mind tools like social media. Can you imagine what he would say today?

If he could see us, as we FaceTime our parents, send a Snapchat to our best friend, tweet our workout routine and send an iMessage to our roommate while we sit on the couch waiting for our delivery.com order? (Just writing that sentence was exhausting, by the way).

Andy, 56, was the first person I talked to when I started writing about how we communicate and his thoughts sounded a lot like what I imagine Mr. Priestley saying.

"Well, to be honest with you Miss, I think the only thing you young folks have mastered is deceit. You keep tweeting tweaking whatever it's called, but you always leave the most important things unsaid. How do y'all sleep at night?"

As offended as I was by Andy's quick assumption that anything we share, post, tweet and tag each other on is actually deceitful, I was also very aware of all the times I posted something to portray an image of myself that might've not been true. #IWokeUpLikeThis posts, anyone?

Although I wanted to, I didn't ask Andy to elaborate, nor could I think of something witty to say back. Instead, I asked a group of twentysomethings to tell me what they thought about it.

"I don't agree. Yeah we tweet about so much bullshit. But we also use social media to make our voice heard on important matters. A lot of us support people like Caitlyn Jenner by communicating like that, you know?" Rob, 26, told me.

His friend, Mary Kate, 27, had a different take.

"I wouldn't go as far as calling us deceitful. We just feel the pressure sometimes. Everyone's life is out there for us to see so we feel like we gotta do the same," she told me.

My good friend, another twenty-two year old freelance writer, sounded surprised when I talked to her about it.

"Deceitful?" she told me over the phone, "We're resourceful, Madda. We just use what we have and we happen to have a lot. Might as well take advantage of it!"

In the months that followed I pretty much heard it all. I went from Millennials who claimed we are skilled and effective communicators to ones who claimed we say a lot without ever saying anything at all.

Bailey, 26, was one of the Millennials I met who tried to elaborate her answer a little bit more.

She asked me if I had an angle for my piece, I told her I did not. She then asked if I was trying to convince my readers of something and I said no.

"I'll be honest then," she started telling me, "Millennials are like a monster with three heads when it comes to communication. It's like there's our real self, and then the phone self and then the professional self. But none of these personas are ever the same."

"What do you mean?" I asked.

"Let me put it this way, a lot of us don't understand the whole 'say what you mean, mean what you say' thing."

Bailey's three-headed monster analogy got me thinking: we do have multiple personalities. Despite having endless means of communication, we tend to be a different version of our self on each one. What we say face-to-face might not be the same as what we message and the emoji we use to go along with that message might have (purposely) more than one meaning.

So back to Andy, I suppose the answer to how we sleep at night is that we tweet about our insomnia hoping our hidden message will, somehow, still go through. Some call it cowardly. I'm pretty sure we call it playing it safe. But, maybe they're the same thing or maybe, it all depends at the head you're looking at.

———————

I'll be the first to point out that if there's one thing Millennials have familiarized themselves with way too much, it is the all-too ambiguous method of communicating solely through the written word, or in some cases, animated emojis or memes.

It was an awful Saturday evening when I dropped, for the umpteenth time, my beloved iPhone5 and cracked my screen. I rushed to the closest T-Mobile store on the Upper East Side and stormed in with the same desperate look a coke-head has when the stash is low.

Charlie, 25, was the unlucky store representative who got to deal with me that day. I mean, I was a damsel in distress, worried about my photos, my notes and my messages. In that exact order. Priorities, people, priorities.

After going through my account information and realizing my insurance did not cover screen damage, Charlie informed me I had to buy a new phone and with that start a new data plan.

"Based on your history, I recommend you get the 6GB high-speed data plan, looks like you don't make a lot of phone calls anyway."

"Actually, I make plenty of phone calls. I need a separate plan for that too," I corrected him.

"Really?" Charlie told me, "I'm looking at your usage here and in the past three months you've sent over 6,000 messages and ran out of data on a monthly basis but only spent about 250 minutes on the phone."

Five hundred dollars and an iPhone6 later, I walked back home and went through all my phone bills only to realize Charlie was not mistaken. Aside from Skype calls, which use data and not minutes, I rarely make any phone calls.

I was in disbelief. How was any of this even possible? I've had a phone since I was about twelve years old and nearly ten years later, I can text, tweet, snap, e-mail and post but can't find the nerve to call someone aside from a select few contacts a.k.a. Mom, Dad and best-friend?

———————————

The next day, I decided to engage in the latest New York City trend: SoulCycle, also known as, spinning your ass off.

I was awkwardly hanging out in the locker room when Sarah, 24, and Miriam, 23, walked in, juice in hand (but of course), gossiping about their Saturday night.

"So he like tried to call me last night and I'm just like, who even does that anymore?" Miriam said.

"Did you pick up?" her friend asked.

"Of course not. I sent him a message and told him to text me instead."

I barged in their conversation and asked why.

"Ugh, phone calls are way too invasive. I need time to think about things before I respond," Sarah said.

"Totally. I only pick up phone calls from family members or work. When people call, I always think, 'Am I supposed to drop everything I'm doing to listen to what you have to say because you decided you have time to say it now?'" Miriam finished.

In a way, I wasn't all that surprised. I mean, clearly, I operated the same way as Charlie had so nicely pointed out.

The more I thought about it, the more I realized that the thing about phone calls is that they require for someone to think on their feet. It's an immediate dialogue. It cannot be crafted, edited, revised, deleted and re-posted. We Millennials aren't used to any of that.

We went from AIM to MSN Messenger to texting to social media. All platforms that give us the time to read words, uncover hidden meanings (if any) and come up with a reply that embodies everything we feel the need to express.

No wonder we don't pick up phone calls. If you think about it, we are less practiced than any other generation when it comes to communicating face-to-face or ear-to-ear.

———————————

At the end of the day, communication comes down to two things: what's being said versus what's being heard. We measure how good or bad our communication skills are by determining how well what we said matches with what was heard.

Phone phobia aside (or telephobia, it's a real thing, look it up!), Millennials have it together when it comes to communicating in the workplace. We have no problem voicing our opinion, thoughts, needs and wants and what we say usually matches what others hear. Whether we do it at appropriate times or not is a whole different story.

But when it comes to relationships, and that includes friendships too, we have grown accustomed to indirect responses. It's not so much about what we're saying versus what's being heard anymore, but it's more about what we're implying versus what others are hearing and understanding.

I'm not sure why, but we seem to like to communicate ambiguously and older generations are our complete opposites, hence all the criticism.

Previous generations are all about functionality and practicality. Our parents often wonder: why email someone when you can call them? Why send someone a picture when you can meet them and show it to them? Why have a Snapchat story showing bits and pieces of your day? What are you trying to communicate to your peers?

To that, I have found, Millennials seldom have an answer. Open, clear communication might not be our specialty but I think you can trust that at least one of those three heads is in fact, saying something worth hearing. It's just a matter of paying attention.

7 THIS IS HOW WE DATE

We didn't change the game. We just changed the rules, and while we were at it, we changed the timing of things too.

In our book, the guy doesn't have to text first. A first date dinner can be replaced with drinks at 10:00 p.m., although midnight totally works too. A potential partner will have our digits before anything else. Their Snapchat story will tell us what they had for lunch before we meet up and the fights we have will be just as public as our selfies.

Consider the following scenario to understand how some of us initiate the dating process.

Part I: The Encounter

Ew chicken legs; swipe left. Yale grad? Nice! Swipe right. Awesome, it's a match! Smoker? Nope, left. Damn, she looks hot in that dress; definitely right. Another match?! Lemme hit her up.

Part II: Setting Up a Date

Her: what brings u to NYC all the way from San Diego?

Him: tbh the cold weather! Hbu? R u from here?

Her: born and raised

Him: maybe u could show me around one of these days?

Her: where do u work?

Him: FiDi, u?

Her: me too! Wanna meet up on wed for a drink and a stroll?

Him: Sure! Whats ur Instagram name? I'll DM[2] u my # ☺

Her: ok ;)

Part III: Making It Official

Your Mom: What do you mean you met online?

---

[2] DM: stands for Direct Message also known as one's private inbox on Instagram, not visible to other followers.

This scenario might look and sound familiar. It is, after all, one of the ways Millennials manage to set up five dates a week from the comfort of their desk or roommate's sofa.

With the help of Tinder, Bumble, OkCupid, Match.com, Grindr and many more, we found a whole new way to date. Unfortunately though, our swiping habits have also enforced the belief we are a hook-up generation.

Apparently, none of us know nor follow proper dating etiquette, whatever that might be, and we date for the sole purpose of hooking-up and kicking people to the curb afterwards.

———————————

I was stuck on the 1 train when I overheard the following conversation between two women:

"I just don't understand. They treat each other like pieces of meat," one woman said to the other.

"Oh, if I catch my daughter on one of those apps she's dead. She should meet a gentleman the good old fashion way," the other one responded.

As I stood there, pretending to listen to music, I started thinking about what the good old fashion way is.

Is there a right or wrong way to go about dating? Should I tell my friends they should be ashamed of swiping left and right? Should we be sticking to meeting people at a bar or walking down the street? Meeting at the office, maybe? Is that old fashion enough?

Should a girl expect a knight in shining armor to show up at her doorstep and sweep her off her feet? And should a guy expect to meet his future wife, equipped with cooking skills, healthy child bearing ovaries and a good sense of humor, while he's watching the game with his bros?

That's not how we do it and, surprise surprise, we're not ashamed of it either.

Online dating might not be my preferred method but, like many others I have tried it. Did I find my Prince Charming? Not really, no. But I didn't catch a sexually transmitted disease, end up roofied at a rave party or murdered in an alley either.

Here's where most parents go, "You got lucky! That's why!"

Online dating and how safe or unsafe it might be, has nothing to do with luck. It has everything to do with common sense, and common sense has nothing to do with which generation you are part of. Let's just say that, some people have it, and others, well, they're still working on it.

I spotted Crystal, 24, cuddling with her girlfriend on the steps of the post office on 34th Street and 8th Avenue.

"We met on Tinder and clicked right away, neither one of us was looking for a hook-up. I felt weird about it at first though. Like, if you think about it, your first impression is based on a photo and we swipe left or right. But then again, I feel like we do the same thing offline. Don't we?"

Yes, Crystal, you are right. In fact, us swiping left or right, isn't any different than our grandparents scanning a room and deciding who they wanted to "get to know better."

First impressions and making a move based on looks is, as shallow as it sounds, human nature. The only difference with Millennials is that we happen to make those decisions through the screen of a phone.

I don't know which part of that deems us at fault, but I do know that if you have a better way, we are all ears. Chances are, we will listen to what you have to say about dating. We'll just swipe left if we don't agree with you and carry on.

———————

A while later, I met Darion, 58, on the elevator of an office building on Park Avenue and 19th Street.

"Looks like it's all physical with you guys," he told me, "Are you all this sex crazed?"

I wouldn't have thought much about Darion's take on the matter if it wasn't for the fact I got a similar response from another thirty something people in the days that followed.

I'd always assumed the perception all Millennials care about is sex was the opinion of a few worried parents, not a widespread belief, but I was starting to reconsider.

Sammy, a twenty-five year old Brand Manager, described how she dates as follows: "I limit emotional attachment but I'm always upfront about it. I'm just too busy being me right now, it wouldn't be fair to the other person."

Her friend, Cassy, added, "I'm sure my mom and pops did the same, we just don't know about it. Anyway, I don't worry too much because everyone craves sex, as long as we're safe about it, don't see where the problem is."

Although Sammy's and Cassy's dating habits were a bit too rough for my taste, their ways certainly didn't make me think they were nymphomaniacs and spinning out of control.

If anything, Sammy especially, made me more conscious of the fact that, despite appearances, we are not at all sex crazed.

Sure, we'll engage in the casual hook-up, but let's not act like we invented one-night stands; those have been around long before us.

We don't crave sex because we're Millennials or because of a dating app or a website. We crave it because we are human beings. I'd even go as far as saying that we crave it just as much as our parents, grandparents and great-grandparents did. I mean, none of us would be here if they didn't, right?

So maybe, instead of labeling Millennials as the "Hook-up Generation" we should just label society. In fact, how does the "Hook-up Society" sound?

"I don't even know who I am yet, never mind who I want to be with. Isn't that what dating is for, anyway?" Sammy told me before hopping on her train.

Yes Sammy, pretty sure it is, indeed.

Dozens of interviews later, I noticed that, regardless of sex or sexual orientation, a lot of twentysomethings share a mindset, or better yet, an attitude, when it comes to dating.

We'll meet someone, in real life or cyber space, and we'll immediately put ourselves on a pedestal. Instead of coming up with reasons why we want to date that person, we come up with all the reasons why they should want to date us.

We start thinking things like, "Why wouldn't this person want to date me? I'm amazing for x, y and z reasons!"

Those of us in our early twenties especially, often fool the other party leading them to believe we know exactly what our self-worth is and what we want.

But really, most of the times, all we're doing is masking our insecurities with confidence. Let's face it, between the ages of 20 and 26 most of us are rocking in an awkward limbo.

We are somewhere in between knowing nothing and everything at the same time. But we seldom admit any of that in the dating field. We're too arrogant to do that.

Instead, we set very high standards, take our confidence up a notch and apply a self-centered mindset to our dating approach. That, if anything, should be the real talk behind how Millennials date. That all too common mindset of "I love myself so much, so why shouldn't you?"

M.J, 24, compared our dating routine to ordering food on Seamless or Delivery.com.

"We have so many choices, if someone messes up our order we won't order from them again. We'll just find some other place. Our generation isn't familiar with scarcity, we have a lot of everything. Dating is no exception."

A few blocks over, I met Brooke, 25.

"I Google all my dates, I just don't want to waste time with someone who doesn't have a job or at least a side project. Nobody has time for that," she said.

M.J and Brooke weren't the only ones operating under this train of thought. I took a stroll down memory lane and thought about my own dating habits and quickly recognized when and how I had behaved the same way.

It dawned on me then, that everyone is so busy speculating on the tools Millennials use to date, that very few people have noticed that the real controversy behind how we date has to do with our unrealistic and demanding expectations.

We were raised surrounded by people who made us think we can always have more, achieve more, and be more. Our childhood was filled with "nothing is impossible" speeches and we somehow managed to apply that slogan to our dating life.

As M.J. pointed out, we don't like to compromise too much, hence the constant bouncing around.

So when it comes to dating, this would be the only behavior I took note of that's really worth mentioning and discussing.

Most of us don't have our shit together but we expect our date to have it all figured out. We don't know who we are, but assume the other person does. We go through something, whether it's a career shift or a personal matter and start to have demands the other person simply can't meet.

We want them to be there for us although we have no idea how we want them to do that. It's like, all of a sudden, we need that one person to fill six different roles in our life. Be my friend! Be my lover! Be my cheerleader! Fulfill my sexual needs! Console me! Motivate me! Laugh with me! Cry with me! Give me mystery! But also give me stability!

We have a tendency to ask for too much too soon and when we don't get it, we move on to something else right away. There's so much supply out there, why bother?

We're impatient and forget all too soon that the people we date are going through our same struggles.

So forget about the dating apps and the websites and the casual hook-ups. That's not unique to our generation.

Want to talk about how we date? Let's start from the very beginning.

8 THIS IS HOW WE CARE

A very perky eight year old boy once told me that when you care about someone you should buy them ice-cream. His sister, two years younger, told me that when you care about someone (or something, she added) you should just talk about them or it all the time until "Mommy sends you to bed because you're talking too much."

I'm not sure why an eight year old and a six year old were able to tell me how they would show someone they care in less than a minute, but the hundreds of Millennials I interviewed had no idea how to answer the same question.

Saki, 22, and his grandmother Nora, 71, suggested the problem wasn't *who* I was asking the question to, but *how* I was asking it.

"You can't just ask people that," Saki told me, "What does 'care' even mean? What do you mean by that?"

Nora quickly supported his statement, "It's going to be hard to write about that, my dear. You have to be clear. Care about what? Care for who?"

Obviously, as the stubborn Millennial that I am, I disregarded their observations and persevered with my method. I figured, if a kid can answer the question, a Millennial can too.

_____

The following Sunday, I asked forty-three young men and women, "How do you care?" purposely not specifying about what.

Forty-two people out of those forty-three started telling me about their job, their studies, their hopes and their dreams for the future and their possessions. One of them, even told me that, "Our generation cares about, like, phone apps" and he wasn't joking.

It was frustrating, and in a way disappointing, to realize that about 98% of the Millennials interviewed in one day, didn't even understand the question.

Instead of telling me how they cared, they gave me a list of what they cared about. But Ray, 23, was my outlier of the day, my two-percent if you will.

"I think we suck at it all. We're too self-centered," he said.

"How so?" I asked.

He raised his eyebrow at me, "When's the last time you told someone you care about them?"

Caught off guard, I was trying to come up with an answer when he added, "And fights do not count. Telling someone you care only when they demand that from you, doesn't count. It means you already failed."

"I guess I don't remember," I responded.

"And I guess I rest my case," he told me as he walked away.

Ray's words lingered in my mind for days. Was he right? Is our generation, the infamous "Me Generation", too self-centered to express care for someone, something, anything really?

———————————

Later that week, I started looking for answers in Brooklyn and that's where I met Luis, 24.

"Why you asking me questions I don't got no answer to?"

"I'm just trying to understand Luis," I said.

"There's nothing for you to understand. We think a lot and we do a lot. The problem is that we never do what we think 'bout and always do what we don't think 'bout. That's how we fuck shit up. And then our mom be like, what's wrong with you young people?"

"So do you think people our age don't know how to care?" I asked him, still confused as to what his take was.

"I'm saying that nobody would be questioning how we do anything if we didn't post shit everywhere. Nobody ever asks my mom how she cares 'bout her job or her husband. You know why? Some of her friends probably don't even know she got a husband!"

I laughed, and although I wasn't sure how Luis's words applied to how we cared yet, I took note of them anyway and walked away.

About an hour later, I was still wandering – fine, I actually got lost – somewhere on the border of Brooklyn and Queens and decided to Uber my way back to Manhattan.

I ended up pooling my ride with Ezra, 26, headed my same direction. With Ray's words still floating around my head, I asked Ezra if he thought people our age were too self-centered to care.

"Here's the deal," Ezra began, "We're really good at caring about practical stuff like careers or causes. We're a savvy and knowledgeable generation. But when it comes to people, not so much. It's not so obvious when we care, I think."

Ezra's argument sounded a lot like Annabelle's, 25, the second to last person I spoke to.

"It all depends on what you're talking about. We show we care about our career by having a vision and working on it every day. We show we care about a cause by using all the tools available to us to make our voice heard," she said.

"And what about people, Annabelle?"

"Isn't that a loaded question? I don't know, I feel like it's different with people. We care like anyone else would but we don't share it as much. I mean yeah, we're GenY, but even tech-savvy people like us don't like to display personal business out there, for everyone to see, you know what I mean?" Annabelle told me.

I recognized then that, although Ray might've been right when he said we're self-centered, Luis, Ezra and Annabelle showed me the flip side of the coin.

The only reason why Millennials are scrutinized so much is because it's so easy to type our name and dig up profiles. It's a double-edged sword.

What we share works in our favor just as much as it works against us. It shows enough to allow people to label us, but not enough to allow people to really know us.

I think that, as much as we love technology, we are still allowed to be conservative in some areas of our life. Maybe when it comes to showing care or affection, it's not only about what we share but also about what we don't.

I should admit that Saki and Nora were right when they told me it was going to be no easy task to write about how Millennials care.

I really did have a hard time, but it wasn't because my questions weren't specific or clear enough. It was because, when I first started, I didn't think about how hard it was going to be. In fact, I don't think any of the people I worked with had planned for it to be this hard.

To make sense of everything going on underneath the surface or below sea level, where it's harder to breakdown actions, feelings and their consequences turned out to be a pretty daunting task.

On top of that, I hadn't even considered the fine, yet distinct line, between love and care, and how the two feelings can often be intertwined, used loosely or even interchangeably, especially amongst Millennials. You'll often catch us substituting "I love you" with "I care about you" and vice versa.

I have found that – yes – we are fickle but that doesn't mean we are careless altogether.

I was asking Millennials a question based on the widespread claim that "Generation Y doesn't care about anything, other than themselves" and I wanted to discredit that so much that I just assumed everyone's definition to care was like mine. But, what if it isn't?

I was taught that the difference between love and care is that love is selfless and never self-serving whereas care, can be a little bit of both. But just because I think you can care without loving but can't love without caring, doesn't mean every other Millennial out there functions that way.

Can care be open to interpretation? If so, should Millennials really be labeled careless, as we often are?

9 THIS IS HOW WE BAIL

There's something to be said about how our generation ends things, bails, parts ways, breaks up – whatever you want to call it. Quite simply, our #BAE[3] can go from being our #MCM[4] or #WCW to our #TBT[5] real fast.

I approached Collin, 26, on a Wednesday evening. I had been walking all over Downtown Manhattan and Brooklyn for hours, asking people how they ended relationships, whatever they interpreted that to mean.

I was pretty inspired with the conversations I'd already had so I wasn't necessarily looking for more, but something drew me to Collin. Maybe his bad boy demeanor.

---

[3] Bae: stands for 'Before Anything Else', commonly used as a hashtag to refer to a significant other.

[4] MCM/WCW: stands for 'Man Crush Monday' or 'Woman Crush Wednesday, trending hashtags used on Mondays and Wednesdays to refer to one's man or woman crush.

[5] TBT: stands for 'Throwback Thursday', trending hashtag used on Thursdays referring to a past event.

"I don't wanna talk to no writer," were his very first words to me when I introduced myself.

Generally speaking, the people who don't want to talk to you, are usually the ones who have the most interesting things to say. So, I insisted.

"Why not?"

"I don't wanna talk to nobody about nothin'," he said.

Feeling particularly risqué that day, I insisted again.

"I just want to have a friendly chat. You don't have to tell me anything you don't want to share," I said as I was already sitting next to him.

Two hours later, I was still there, talking to someone who, as it turned out, had a lot to say, despite claiming otherwise.

In fact, what happened between Collin and I, wasn't even a dialogue. It was more of a soliloquy, starring pretty much himself.

He started out by telling me about his recent breakup. It was nothing I hadn't heard before. What he was calling a misunderstanding, his girlfriend deemed as cheating and, just like that, it was over.

"I don't think the problem is how we bail Maddalena," he told me.

"So what is it then?"

"We [are] all cowards but that's okay 'cus we [are] young and have that excuse till we're thirty maybe. The real problem is that even when we end things, we never really do. I don't know how you gonna write about this shit when, people like me and you, don't know how to end things."

"I'm not sure what you mean by that," I responded.

"I dunno, I'm just sayin'. Aren't you a writer? Isn't it your job to figure that out?"

I transcribed his last few thoughts in my notebook and as I traveled back to Manhattan on an overcrowded L train, I accepted the fact I had no idea what Collin meant by that. Little did I know, I would find out soon enough.

———————

A few weeks later, I was standing in line at Juice Press in the Upper West Side when I ran into Jason, 25, a friend of a friend. We hadn't seen each other in a while so we spent some time catching up.

He told me about his trip to Thailand and his recent entrepreneurial ventures. When I asked how his girlfriend was doing he told me they had recently broken up.

"Sorry to hear. Give it time, maybe you guys can patch things up," I reassured him.

"I don't think so, Madda. Pretty sure she hates my guts," he confessed as he reached out for his juice.

I figured this would be a good time to mention what I was working on and Jason agreed to tell me how he bailed on his ex-girlfriend.

"I ghosted. I stuck around long enough for her to care and then I disappeared," he told me.

"What'd you do that for?"

"She's a good person. I'm not. Better get outta there before she realized that."

Jason reminded me of Roco, 86, the oldest person I interviewed while working on this project. I had originally approached him to ask him about how Generation Y travels and this is what he told me:

"I retired a long time ago. I don't know how you work or travel or any of these other topics you are writing about. But I will tell you this, sometimes you young people scare the crap out of me! When I asked my daughter why she broke up with that nice man she told me it was horrifying to care for someone more than she cared about herself. Tell me, is that what's horrifying to you guys? You know what's horrifying to me? If I Google her name more than fifty-five pictures come up. Anyone could have her information but she's not worried about that. Ah to be young and stupid."

At the time, I didn't have a comeback so I didn't say anything. But after talking to Jason and a few others I started to put two and two together.

Jason has 1.2k followers on Instagram and Twitter. He's a fine gentleman; fit, healthy, financially stable, successful career. On paper, or better yet, on cyberspace, he seems to have a pretty sweet life.

Roco's daughter isn't any different. From what he told me about her she is just as healthy and successful as Jason.

I then thought about myself and how, after talking to Roco, I immediately went home, googled my name and took down some pretty horrifying things I had forgotten about. What I didn't do, however, was call the first person I thought about while Roco was lecturing me.

Jason bailed. Roco's daughter bailed. I bailed. And most of the twentysomethings I met, bailed in similar ways too.

That's when it dawned on me that maybe, our cockiness and perceived arrogance is just that, a perception. Maybe, behind our perfect Instagram accounts and carefully crafted tweets, we're just as insecure as any other generation. Sometimes so much so that we trick ourselves out of love. We bail on others not realizing the only person we are really bailing on is our own self.

"I hope she reads your book," Jason told me before I walked out, "Maybe, she'll give me another chance."

See? Chickens, we're such chickens. And good call Roco, sometimes we really are young and stupid.

Months later, as I was listening to my tape recorder again, I found a common denominator in everyone's responses.

Every young man and woman I met had admitted they didn't think twice before breaking bonds with their girlfriend, boyfriend or significant almost partner/fuckbuddy/who needs labels anyway.

Whatever the reason was - be it cheating, fear of commitment, selfishness and many more -

none of them had even considered the possibility that their relationship might be worth fighting for. The only solution they came up with was ending it and moving on to something else. But did they really? End it, that is?

Most people, admitted they kept track of the other person the only way we Millennials know and that got me thinking back to what Collin told me.

When our grandparents or parents would go through a breakup, they had no way (or very limited ways) to keep track of the other person. Once it was over, it was over. Unless they met casually around town or through friends of friends, chances were, they would never hear from or see that person ever again unless struck from some sort of serendipity moment.

But, with Generation Y, things aren't quite like that.

Even after we leave, even after we walk away, even after we bail on people, we still know a whole lot about them.

We'll read their Twitter feed, check their Instagram, watch their Snapchat story and keep an eye on their Facebook check-ins. That's right: we become the big brother.

Sometimes we get so caught up in this behavior that we have the audacity to judge the other person's life choices based on what we see online even if we know all too well that what's displayed online could be misleading.

Was that what Collin meant? Maybe this, is how Generation Y bails, breaks up, parts ways.

We become strangers to one another. But not just any type of stranger. We become the type of stranger who will occasionally like your photo. The type of stranger who knows when you're on a trip somewhere. The type of stranger whose friends will text as soon as you post a picture with somebody else, somebody that isn't you.

We become the type of stranger who will distance him or herself enough from someone but never too far to not be able to reach out in the future. Because, the way we see it, you never know and in our twenties, we never really do know.

10 THIS IS HOW WE LOVE

Fact: I never intended to write about how we love. Great philosophers, authors, scientists and psychologists haven't been able to come up with an actual answer yet and I certainly wasn't planning on taking on that sort of challenge. But I changed my mind at 5:30 a.m. on a random Friday.

I was going through news articles, op-eds and book excerpts, when I found an article in The New York Times that forced me to reconsider my decision.

The headline read, "Love, Actually" and the sub-headline, "Teaching Generation Y the Basics of a Strong Relationship." Written by Professor Reiner, a Townson University professor, the article appeared in print on February 9th, 2014, coincidentally right around the corner from Valentine's Day.

So much annoyed me about it. From the claim that hooking up and hanging out is our "romance operandi" to the one that assumed we are unprepared for marriage to the one that alleged sex is the center of our identity.

There was one sentence though that just hit home.

"For this resume-driven generation, schools would do well to add a grade-based seminar about love. The course could cross many academic disciplines: the biology of intimacy; the multicultural history of courtship; the psychology and sociology of vulnerability." Professor Reiner writes.

Although, in his final remarks, he did admit his proposition might have been a bit far-fetched, it didn't really change the fact his whole piece was based on the assumption Millennials don't feel love, can't be intimate and don't allow themselves to be vulnerable with one another.

On a napkin, I made a list of people I have loved in the past, people I love to this day and I even added, people I hope to love someday and how I plan to do so. I then thought about the people close to me and identified how they loved too and as I read the article over and over again, I started questioning it more and more.

Can love be taught? If so, who would be qualified enough to teach it to us? Divorced parents? Would it be taught in schools too or just universities and colleges? Who would be writing the syllabus? The same people who opposed same-sex marriage? How would the grading work?

By 8:00 a.m. that morning, I had bought a brand new notebook and changed the batteries of my recorder: I was going to be writing about how we love, after all.

A sad truth soon emerged: Professor Reiner was no outlier. If anything, he was one of the many. On the streets of New York City, there seemed to be plenty of people who shared his view.

The truth hurts baby and that day I faced the harsh reality that when it comes to love, our reputation precedes us. We are known to be a reckless generation and we are especially known, for being reckless with each other's feelings.

I met Josh, 23, on a sunny Saturday afternoon. He was standing outside a pre-war building, waiting for his friend to come downstairs. I asked him the same questions I asked the twenty-five men and women I met before him that day.

"How does our generation love Josh? How do you love?" While most people had hesitated before coming up with an answer, Josh spoke up immediately.

"Fast. We're intense. But you don't see many us sticking around for too long. It's too much pressure. Aside from my family and friends, I have genuinely loved a lot of people. Doesn't mean I stayed with them. Am I dick?"

Well, cough, cough.

Three days later, I was having coffee at Maison Kayser in the Flatiron District and met Jennifer, 25. She was sitting at the table next to me and was on the phone with whom, I could only assume, was a close friend of hers.

Based on what Jennifer was saying, it was pretty obvious that whoever was on the other line was going through a breakup and Jennifer was giving him or her the typical, "he's not good enough for you, you deserve better" speech.

When she hung-up the phone, I asked her the same question I'd asked Josh.

"I once had a boyfriend who refused to post our pictures," Jennifer started telling me.

"We broke up shortly after, he didn't know how to show love and –"

"Oh c'mon," I interrupted her, "You can't measure someone's feelings like that."

"You're right. But you can tell when someone is trying to hide. People don't hide someone they claim to love, especially people our age. If anything, when we love, we want everyone to know. Love is all about sharing. Social media is just a way. I was right about him too. A few months later, I found out he was seeing somebody else simultaneously. Told ya, such a sketchy motherfucker."

That night, as I went through my notes, I started thinking that maybe Josh was right, we aren't capable of fully committing to someone.

I mean, why would we? We can barely commit to an apartment, a phone carrier or a career path.

But Jennifer had a point too. Maybe people shouldn't be fooled by the fact we hide our feelings behind a double tap, a share, a post, a snap or 140 characters. It might not be the best of ways, but maybe, that's our way.

"It's superficial to show love like that," our parents tells us as we post a picture with someone important to us. But then again, our parents would page 1-4-3 on their beepers to say 'I love you.' Our grandparents had to resort to handwritten letters. So what's the difference, really?

Maybe if our grandparents had had the opportunity back then to hashtag their feelings, they would've done so too.

Isn't that the point, anyway? To show love the only way you know how to?

Most people assume the chances of running into someone you know in an overcrowded city like New York are slim to none. But you'd be surprised, if you pay enough attention that is, how many times you can cross paths with the same strangers.

That's exactly what happened to me with Jamie and his daughter, Carolina.

I met Jamie, 48, for the first time in April and I was immediately intrigued by him. I was sitting on a bench enjoying bearable temperatures after having suffered through a glacial winter, when I saw him walk out of New York University's Welcome Center on West 4th Street.

He was with Carolina, 23, and holding pamphlets, brochures and stickers. He was wearing a smirk; that same smirk parents usually have when they see something they'd love their child to be part of.

"You heard what the counselor said, your GPA is good and you've been involved in the paper long enough. You have very good chances of getting in," I overheard him tell her.

"I guess," she responded, as she grabbed one of the pamphlets and started flicking through the pages.

It was obvious to me that Jamie was a lot more excited about NYU than Carolina and although I didn't know what their circumstances were exactly, that interaction between a father and a daughter was something I was very familiar with.

When I finally decided to walk towards them, Carolina stepped away to buy a snack at a nearby kiosk, so I ended up speaking to Jamie first.

"She lives in Boston but is looking to transfer. It's hard to help her. She doesn't know what she wants to do. She wanted to take a year off which I am absolutely against. A year for what? Wishful thinking?" he asked me, as if I could answer that for him.

When Carolina returned, Jamie told her he had to head back to work.

"I think I'm going to take a walk on the Hudson," she told him, "I'll see you home, Dad."

As soon as Jamie left, Carolina and I walked a few blocks together.

"Just find what you love and do a lot of it," I told her, assuming her problem was not knowing which career path to take.

"That's not it. He's given me everything a girl could possibly ask for and I love him so much. But, I don't want to be in New York or Boston. I want to move to Spain, for a year, with my boyfriend. I love him, too. But my Dad doesn't see it that way, he doesn't think a 23 year old knows anything about love."

I immediately jumped on the opportunity to investigate further.

"How do you love, Carolina?"

Her response was so detailed and well thought that I felt like she had been rehearsing it for months, maybe even years, just waiting for someone, perhaps her father, to finally ask her how she loved. Her words were inspiring and worth every minor hand cramp I got as I was writing as fast as I could in my notebook.

The more I listened to her tell me how she loves her dad, her boyfriend, her passions – her life basically – the more I kept thinking about that article and how inaccurate it really was. I couldn't wait to sit down and write something based on what Carolina was telling me.

But she called me the next morning at 4:30 a.m. to tell me she had changed her mind and didn't want me to quote her. I tore up my notes and although I couldn't publish her thoughts, there was no way I was going to forget her words.

She's one of the few twentysomethings I spoke to who didn't mention the digital age and how it has affected us. She talked about everything but technology and reminded me that, contrary to popular belief, we still feel feelings and think things and do stuff.

Just like twentysomething me. Just like fortysomething Jamie. Basically, just like you, however old you are.

———————————

Nearly one month later, I was rushing down Seventh Avenue when I ran into Jamie again, this time alone. He didn't mention anything about Spain so neither did I.

I assumed, Carolina still hadn't figured out a way to tell the father she loves, what she was planning to do with the man she is in love with. As much as I wanted to ask, I knew it was not my place to tell Jamie about what Carolina and I had discussed.

Before going back to the human stampede that was Seventh Avenue that day, I offered him some advice.

I advised him to look closer. I suggested that maybe he wasn't seeing the big picture. He was blaming her for not knowing; for being lost; for taking a break. The picture of her life was looking blurry to him. Not sharp enough for a father to fully understand his daughter. Ultimately, I tried to remind him that, even when pictures are blurry, you can still recognize objects.

"See that, Jamie?" I told him, "That might be her passion and that might be her fear, and that over there, might be what she'll end up doing five years from now. You don't know, but if you just look closer, you might find out."

I would advise the Professor Reiner's of the world to do the same.

Honestly, someone telling us we don't know how to love feels a lot like being bullied in the hallway by the older kids. It fools us into believing that older generations – generations that aren't featured in books, newspaper articles, TV shows and debates and that aren't looked at through a magnifying glass – actually do know how to love and we twentysomethings aren't working hard enough to learn from them.

So with this feeling in mind, I have two options; I could wrap this essay up in one of two ways.

On the one hand, I could keep going and share the thoughts of the other 226 Millennials I spoke to.

I could guide you through their thoughts and share with you over one hundred different ways in which we love, hoping that at least one of those ways resonates with you and defeats the stigma around Millennials and love once and for all.

I am not going to go with that option though. If I did, I would only be validating the claim we aren't capable of true, real, love and that's the last thing I want to do. I refuse to sit here and speculate on a claim I already know is farce.

I am going to go with option two instead. I will leave you with something that summarizes the underlying message behind those 226 responses I collected and will allow you to draw your own conclusions from there.

This is what I'll leave you with.

Love goes hand in hand with fear. The minute we fall in love with someone we automatically acquire the fear of losing it. Fear can drive people to do stupid, crazy, irrational, [insert here your word of choice] actions. Those actions are the same actions that allow outsiders – witnesses of that love – to label, judge or criticize one's way of loving.

If we all decide to believe that the above is true, then I don't really have to give you an answer to how Millennials love, do I? You already have it, no matter how young or old you are.

You can find your answer by tapping into your own feelings of love towards someone.

Ask yourself this: What actions did you take that you couldn't explain to yourself, never mind others, because of love? What did you say, that didn't make sense to outsiders? What did you feel when someone told you your love wasn't valid? What was your way to love? And how many people did you blame for not understanding who, what and how you were loving?

Whatever your answer to these questions is, that's how we love. That's our answer too because when it comes to love, we are just like anyone else. We are just like you.

And if you can't think of an answer, then consider the possibility that maybe, the one who doesn't know how to love is not Generation Y.

11 & THIS IS HOW I LIVE

I guess I should start this last piece with a confession. What you're holding in your hands or reading from your Kindle or iSomething gadget was never planned or premeditated.

I tried writing a book with that approach before and I utterly failed. I worked on a fiction novel for two years and I ended up tossing it out because I couldn't figure out an ending.

It didn't occur to me until now, that the reason why I was never able to finish that manuscript is because at the time, I was motivated by all the wrong things.

I wasn't writing because I had something to say or because I wanted to be heard. I was forcing myself to write because I was after some sort of hype. The hype of calling myself an author. The hype of feeling like I had accomplished something tangible. The hype of cashing in royalties. But this book didn't start like that. It didn't start like that at all.

On the contrary, up to nine months ago, this was a blank word document I opened on a cold February night at 2:00 a.m.

I typed in the words, "This Is How It Goes" and I went on a full blown rant about everything: school, work, family, friends, boyfriends and finances.

At the time, I was feeling overwhelmed. I was feeling lost. But above all, I was feeling stuck. I couldn't figure out what I wanted to do, who I wanted to be, where I wanted to go and how I was going to get there. That night, I wrote and wrote and wrote until I finally passed out.

The following morning I woke up to a hangover and over ten pages of complaints.

With a strong cup of joe and two Advil in hand, I read over everything I had written and started to contemplate the possibility that maybe I wasn't alone.

There's just no way I'm the only person feeling like shit right now, I kept thinking to myself.

I mean, don't get me wrong, I think I'm cool and everything, but I'm not *that* special.

I decided to send my piece, also known as my semi-drunken rant, to my editor and hear her thoughts. I figured that sharing it or at the very least reading my work out loud to someone would make me feel something; possibly something like less alone.

Since I didn't want my editor to think I was borderline suicidal though, I only shared two pages out of the ten I had handy. Those two pages happened to be about Millennials and breakups.

Fast-forward to two weeks later, we polished those two pages and published, "This Is How It Ends."

Suddenly I didn't feel so alone anymore. People were relating to my writing. People who had gone through or were going through the same things. Those people had my same thoughts, my same feelings. They too, were navigating a pool of emotions and had no idea what to do with themselves.

I started thinking, that if people could relate to my piece about a breakup, in retrospect something so temporary and in the big scheme of things almost trivial, maybe they would relate to all that other "stuff" I was ranting about too.

That moment right then and there, was when I first started this project. I call it a project because that's exactly what it was to me at the time, it wasn't a book just yet.

I decided to focus on topics that, whether we want to admit it or not, we all think about every day because they are the foundation on which we build our lives: love, money and career.

I wanted people to truly trust me and feel safe confiding in me, hence the anonymity of the individuals interviewed.

At the same time, I also wanted to fight preconceived notions surrounding people our age; notions I kept hearing and reading about everywhere I went.

I wanted to stand up for myself and others. I wanted to be an advocate, yes, but not as much as I wanted to understand us twentysomethings, in the hope that maybe, I could understand something about myself too.

Soon enough, the streets of New York City became my research lab. I started talking to anyone who was willing to share thoughts, feelings, stories and opinions and I listened to every single person very carefully.

A few months and something like twelve Moleskine notebooks later, I put together these essays. And that's when my project became a book and #ThisIsHowWeLive came to life.

This book became my therapy. It was my way to cope with all the wonderful but often confusing turns life takes. It was never meant to be a book. To be honest, it was never meant to be shared with anyone at all. It was supposed to be my collective diary; my consolation; my safe place.

But once I found myself again, I thought back to that cold February night and how alone I felt and how this little project of mine had made me feel alive again.

I remembered a poem a good friend and mentor e-mailed me a few years ago and I particularly remembered the last four words:

"STRIVE TO BE HAPPY." [6]

That's when I decided to publish my collective diary; my therapy; my very own attempt to happiness. I felt that #ThisIsHowWeLive had to be shared, just in case someone else out there

---

[6] A passage from the prose-poem "Desiderata" by American writer Max Ehrmann.

was feeling like I was that night.

If any of this sounds like you, then let this book be your reminder that you are not alone.

If, however, none of this sounds like you, but you read these pieces anyway, then let this book be your reminder that, at the end of the day, when it comes to Generation Y, we're all just a group of people playing in the same playground and aside from sharing toys, swing sets and soccer balls, we also share the same feelings about life. Feelings you most likely felt too at some point in your twenties, regardless of the generation you belong to now.

As far as how I live goes, I now wake up every morning feeling part of a herd. I like to think, I graze around New York City, amongst thousands of other Millennials, feeling different but never feeling alone.

Think of a zebra. I am part of the Generation Y herd and although from afar we all look the same, with black and white stripes on our coat, if you look close enough you'll notice each one of us has a unique striping pattern.

I live every single day knowing that I am part of this herd and that I'm not going through anything someone else, someone from any generation, hasn't gone through and survived already.

If writing this book has taught me anything it is that it's the moments right before you find out what you stand for that are the most electrifying. Those eureka moments. When all of a sudden, you just know what you have to do, how you're going to do it, and why.

Those are the moments I live for now, along with my fellow Millennials, and it really shouldn't matter that much to anyone what we do and how we do it while we wait for that eureka moment to hit us.

This is how I live now and I hope it's going to be how you live too.

#IAmAZebra, are you?

Maddalena, 23
New York City

ABOUT THE AUTHOR

Maddalena Alecce is a writer, editor and marketing communications enthusiast. Born and raised in Milan, Italy she moved to the United States in 2010.
She graduated from the State University of New York, Fashion Institute of Technology, with a degree in Advertising and Marketing Communications and a minor in English Writing.
While in college, Maddalena launched her editorial web-column, *Foreigner in the City*, which chronicled her adventures in New York City.
#ThisIsHowWeLive is her debut non-fiction novel.
Maddalena is 23 and resides in New York City.

Visit www.maddalenaalecce.com
Email: maddalena.alecce@gmail.com
Instagram: @maddanyc
Twitter: @MaddalenaAlecce

26547428R00067

Made in the USA
Middletown, DE
01 December 2015